The Song of

SOLOMON

ISBN 13: 978-1-5154-4099-4

The Song of
SOLOMON

CHAPTER 1

1:1 The song of songs, which [is] Solomon's. 1:2 Let him kiss me with the
kisses of his mouth: for thy love [is] better than wine. 1:3 Because of the
savour of thy good ointments thy name [is as] ointment poured forth,
therefore do the virgins love thee. 1:4 Draw me, we will run after thee: the
king hath brought me into his chambers: we will be glad and rejoice in thee,
we will remember thy love more than wine: the upright love thee. 1:5 I [am]
black, but comely, O ye daughters of Jerusalem, as the tents of Kedar, as the
curtains of Solomon. 1:6 Look not upon me, because I [am] black, because
the sun hath looked upon me: my mother's children were angry with me;
they made me the keeper of the vineyards; [but] mine own vineyard have I
not kept. 1:7 Tell me, O thou whom my soul loveth, where thou feedest,
where thou makest [thy flock] to rest at noon: for why should I be as one that
turneth aside by the flocks of thy companions? 1:8 If thou know not, O thou
fairest among women, go thy way forth by the footsteps of the flock, and feed
thy kids beside the shepherds' tents. 1:9 I have compared thee, O my love,
to a company of horses in Pharaoh's chariots. 1:10 Thy cheeks are comely
with rows [of jewels], thy neck with chains [of gold]. 1:11 We will make thee
borders of gold with studs of silver. 1:12 While the king [sitteth] at his table,
my spikenard sendeth forth the smell thereof. 1:13 A bundle of myrrh [is] my
wellbeloved unto me; he shall lie all night betwixt my breasts. 1:14 My
beloved [is] unto me [as] a cluster of camphire in the vineyards of Engedi.
1:15 Behold, thou [art] fair, my love; behold, thou [art] fair; thou [hast] doves'
eyes. 1:16 Behold, thou [art] fair, my beloved, yea, pleasant: also our bed [is]
green. 1:17 The beams of our house [are] cedar, [and] our rafters of fir.

CHAPTER 2

2:1 I [am] the rose of Sharon, [and] the lily of the valleys. 2:2 As the lily
among thorns, so [is] my love among the daughters. 2:3 As the apple tree
among the trees of the wood, so [is] my beloved among the sons. I sat down
under his shadow with great delight, and his fruit [was] sweet to my taste. 2:4
He brought me to the banqueting house, and his banner over me [was] love.

2:5 Stay me with flagons, comfort me with apples: for I [am] sick of love. 2:6 His left hand [is] under my head, and his right hand doth embrace me. 2:7 I charge you, O ye daughters of Jerusalem, by the roes, and by the hinds of the field, that ye stir not up, nor awake [my] love, till he please. 2:8 The voice of my beloved! behold, he cometh leaping upon the mountains, skipping upon the hills. 2:9 My beloved is like a roe or a young hart: behold, he standeth behind our wall, he looketh forth at the windows, shewing himself through the lattice. 2:10 My beloved spake, and said unto me, Rise up, my love, my fair one, and come away. 2:11 For, lo, the winter is past, the rain is over [and] gone; 2:12 The flowers appear on the earth; the time of the singing [of birds] is come, and the voice of the turtle is heard in our land; 2:13 The fig tree putteth forth her green figs, and the vines [with] the tender grape give a [good] smell. Arise, my love, my fair one, and come away. 2:14 O my dove, [that art] in the clefts of the rock, in the secret [places] of the stairs, let me see thy countenance, let me hear thy voice; for sweet [is] thy voice, and thy countenance [is] comely. 2:15 Take us the foxes, the little foxes, that spoil the vines: for our vines [have] tender grapes. 2:16 My beloved [is] mine, and I [am] his: he feedeth among the lilies. 2:17 Until the day break, and the shadows flee away, turn, my beloved, and be thou like a roe or a young hart upon the mountains of Bether.

CHAPTER 3

3:1 By night on my bed I sought him whom my soul loveth: I sought him, but I found him not. 3:2 I will rise now, and go about the city in the streets, and in the broad ways I will seek him whom my soul loveth: I sought him, but I found him not. 3:3 The watchmen that go about the city found me: [to whom I said], Saw ye him whom my soul loveth? 3:4 [It was] but a little that I passed from them, but I found him whom my soul loveth: I held him, and would not let him go, until I had brought him into my mother's house, and into the chamber of her that conceived me. 3:5 I charge you, O ye daughters of Jerusalem, by the roes, and by the hinds of the field, that ye stir not up, nor awake [my] love, till he please. 3:6 Who [is] this that cometh out of the wilderness like pillars of smoke, perfumed with myrrh and frankincense, with all powders of the merchant? 3:7 Behold his bed, which [is] Solomon's; threescore valiant men [are] about it, of the valiant of Israel. 3:8 They all hold swords, [being] expert in war: every man [hath] his sword upon his thigh because of fear in the night. 3:9 King Solomon made himself a chariot of the wood of Lebanon. 3:10 He made the pillars thereof [of] silver, the bottom thereof [of] gold, the covering of it [of] purple, the midst thereof being paved [with] love, for the daughters of Jerusalem. 3:11 Go forth, O ye daughters of Zion, and behold king Solomon with the crown wherewith his mother crowned him in the day of his espousals, and in the day of the gladness of his heart.

CHAPTER 4

4:1 Behold, thou [art] fair, my love; behold, thou [art] fair; thou [hast] doves' eyes within thy locks: thy hair [is] as a flock of goats, that appear from mount Gilead. 4:2 Thy teeth [are] like a flock [of sheep that are even] shorn, which came up from the washing; whereof every one bear twins, and none [is] barren among them. 4:3 Thy lips [are] like a thread of scarlet, and thy speech [is] comely: thy temples [are] like a piece of a pomegranate within thy locks. 4:4 Thy neck [is] like the tower of David builded for an armoury, whereon there hang a thousand bucklers, all shields of mighty men. 4:5 Thy two breasts [are] like two young roes that are twins, which feed among the lilies. 4:6 Until the day break, and the shadows flee away, I will get me to the mountain of myrrh, and to the hill of frankincense. 4:7 Thou [art] all fair, my love; [there is] no spot in thee. 4:8 Come with me from Lebanon, [my] spouse, with me from Lebanon: look from the top of Amana, from the top of Shenir and Hermon, from the lions' dens, from the mountains of the leopards. 4:9 Thou hast ravished my heart, my sister, [my] spouse; thou hast ravished my heart with one of thine eyes, with one chain of thy neck. 4:10 How fair is thy love, my sister, [my] spouse! how much better is thy love than wine! and the smell of thine ointments than all spices! 4:11 Thy lips, O [my] spouse, drop [as] the honeycomb: honey and milk [are] under thy tongue; and

the smell of thy garments [is] like the smell of Lebanon. 4:12 A garden
inclosed [is] my sister, [my] spouse; a spring shut up, a fountain sealed. 4:13
Thy plants [are] an orchard of pomegranates, with pleasant fruits; camphire,
with spikenard, 4:14 Spikenard and saffron; calamus and cinnamon, with all
trees of frankincense; myrrh and aloes, with all the chief spices: 4:15 A
fountain of gardens, a well of living waters, and streams from Lebanon. 4:16
Awake, O north wind; and come, thou south; blow upon my garden, [that]
the spices thereof may flow out. Let my beloved come into his garden, and
eat his pleasant fruits.

CHAPTER 5

5:1 I am come into my garden, my sister, [my] spouse: I have gathered my
myrrh with my spice; I have eaten my honeycomb with my honey; I have
drunk my wine with my milk: eat, O friends; drink, yea, drink abundantly,
O beloved. 5:2 I sleep, but my heart waketh: [it is] the voice of my beloved
that knocketh, [saying], Open to me, my sister, my love, my dove, my
undefiled: for my head is filled with dew, [and] my locks with the drops of the
night. 5:3 I have put off my coat; how shall I put it on? I have washed my feet;
how shall I defile them? 5:4 My beloved put in his hand by the hole [of the
door], and my bowels were moved for him. 5:5 I rose up to open to my
beloved; and my hands dropped [with] myrrh, and my fingers [with] sweet
smelling myrrh, upon the handles of the lock. 5:6 I opened to my beloved;
but my beloved had withdrawn himself, [and] was gone: my soul failed when
he spake: I sought him, but I could not find him; I called him, but he gave
me no answer. 5:7 The watchmen that went about the city found me, they
smote me, they wounded me; the keepers of the walls took away my veil from
me. 5:8 I charge you, O daughters of Jerusalem, if ye find my beloved, that
ye tell him, that I [am] sick of love. 5:9 What [is] thy beloved more than
[another] beloved, O thou fairest among women? what [is] thy beloved more
than [another] beloved, that thou dost so charge us? 5:10 My beloved [is]
white and ruddy, the chiefest among ten thousand. 5:11 His head [is as] the
most fine gold, his locks [are] bushy, [and] black as a raven. 5:12 His eyes [are]

as [the eyes] of doves by the rivers of waters, washed with milk, [and] fitly set. 5:13 His cheeks [are] as a bed of spices, [as] sweet flowers: his lips [like] lilies, dropping sweet smelling myrrh. 5:14 His hands [are as] gold rings set with the beryl: his belly [is as] bright ivory overlaid [with] sapphires. 5:15 His legs [are as] pillars of marble, set upon sockets of fine gold: his countenance [is] as Lebanon, excellent as the cedars. 5:16 His mouth [is] most sweet: yea, he [is] altogether lovely. This [is] my beloved, and this [is] my friend, O daughters of Jerusalem.

CHAPTER 6

6:1 Whither is thy beloved gone, O thou fairest among women? whither is thy beloved turned aside? that we may seek him with thee. 6:2 My beloved is gone down into his garden, to the beds of spices, to feed in the gardens, and to gather lilies. 6:3 I [am] my beloved's, and my beloved [is] mine: he feedeth among the lilies. 6:4 Thou [art] beautiful, O my love, as Tirzah, comely as Jerusalem, terrible as [an army] with banners. 6:5 Turn away thine eyes from me, for they have overcome me: thy hair [is] as a flock of goats that appear from Gilead. 6:6 Thy teeth [are] as a flock of sheep which go up from the washing, whereof every one beareth twins, and [there is] not one barren among them. 6:7 As a piece of a pomegranate [are] thy temples within thy locks. 6:8 There are threescore queens, and fourscore concubines, and virgins without number. 6:9 My dove, my undefiled is [but] one; she [is] the [only] one of her mother, she [is] the choice [one] of her that bare her. The daughters saw her, and blessed her; [yea], the queens and the concubines, and they praised her. 6:10 Who [is] she [that] looketh forth as the morning, fair as the moon, clear as the sun, [and] terrible as [an army] with banners? 6:11 I went down into the garden of nuts to see the fruits of the valley, [and] to see whether the vine flourished, [and] the pomegranates budded. 6:12 Or ever I was aware, my soul made me [like] the chariots of Amminadib. 6:13 Return, return, O Shulamite; return, return, that we may look upon thee. What will ye see in the Shulamite? As it were the company of two armies.

CHAPTER 7

7:1 How beautiful are thy feet with shoes, O prince's daughter! the joints of thy thighs [are] like jewels, the work of the hands of a cunning workman. 7:2 Thy navel [is like] a round goblet, [which] wanteth not liquor: thy belly [is like] an heap of wheat set about with lilies. 7:3 Thy two breasts [are] like two young roes [that are] twins. 7:4 Thy neck [is] as a tower of ivory; thine eyes [like] the fishpools in Heshbon, by the gate of Bathrabbim: thy nose [is] as the tower of Lebanon which looketh toward Damascus. 7:5 Thine head upon thee [is] like Carmel, and the hair of thine head like purple; the king [is] held in the galleries. 7:6 How fair and how pleasant art thou, O love, for delights! 7:7 This thy stature is like to a palm tree, and thy breasts to clusters [of grapes]. 7:8 I said, I will go up to the palm tree, I will take hold of the boughs thereof: now also thy breasts shall be as clusters of the vine, and the smell of thy nose like apples; 7:9 And the roof of thy mouth like the best wine for my beloved, that goeth [down] sweetly, causing the lips of those that are asleep to speak. 7:10 I [am] my beloved's, and his desire [is] toward me. 7:11 Come, my beloved, let us go forth into the field; let us lodge in the villages. 7:12 Let us get up early to the vineyards; let us see if the vine flourish, [whether] the tender grape appear, [and] the pomegranates bud forth: there will I give thee my loves. 7:13 The mandrakes give a smell, and at our gates [are] all manner of pleasant [fruits], new and old, [which] I have laid up for thee, O my beloved.

CHAPTER 8

8:1 O that thou [wert] as my brother, that sucked the breasts of my mother! [when] I should find thee without, I would kiss thee; yea, I should not be despised. 8:2 I would lead thee, [and] bring thee into my mother's house, [who] would instruct me: I would cause thee to drink of spiced wine of the juice of my pomegranate. 8:3 His left hand [should be] under my head, and his right hand should embrace me. 8:4 I charge you, O daughters of Jerusalem, that ye stir not up, nor awake [my] love, until he please. 8:5 Who [is] this that cometh up from the wilderness, leaning upon her beloved? I

raised thee up under the apple tree: there thy mother brought thee forth:
there she brought thee forth [that] bare thee. 8:6 Set me as a seal upon thine
heart, as a seal upon thine arm: for love [is] strong as death; jealousy [is] cruel
as the grave: the coals thereof [are] coals of fire, [which hath] a most
vehement flame. 8:7 Many waters cannot quench love, neither can the floods
drown it: if a man would give all the substance of his house for love, it would
utterly be contemned. 8:8 We have a little sister, and she hath no breasts:
what shall we do for our sister in the day when she shall be spoken for? 8:9
If she [be] a wall, we will build upon her a palace of silver: and if she [be] a
door, we will inclose her with boards of cedar. 8:10 I [am] a wall, and my
breasts like towers: then was I in his eyes as one that found favour. 8:11
Solomon had a vineyard at Baalhamon; he let out the vineyard unto keepers;
every one for the fruit thereof was to bring a thousand [pieces] of silver. 8:12
My vineyard, which [is] mine, [is] before me: thou, O Solomon, [must have]
a thousand, and those that keep the fruit thereof two hundred. 8:13 Thou
that dwellest in the gardens, the companions hearken to thy voice: cause me
to hear [it]. 8:14 Make haste, my beloved, and be thou like to a roe or to a
young hart upon the mountains of spices.

978-1-5154-4137-3 The First Epistle General of Peter
978-1-5154-4138-0 The Second General Epistle of Peter
978-1-5154-4139-7 The First Epistle General of John
978-1-5154-4140-3 The Second Epistle General of John
978-1-5154-4141-0 The Third Epistle General of John
978-1-5154-4142-7 The General Epistle of Jude
978-1-5154-4143-4 The Revelation of Saint John the Devine

Lightning Source UK Ltd.
Milton Keynes UK
UKHW010626251121
394551UK00001B/41

9 781515 440994